Cars

By Heather Hammonds

T0342781

Contents

Title	Text Type	Pages
Cars Today	Information Report	2–9
Why People Drive Cars	Explanation	10–16

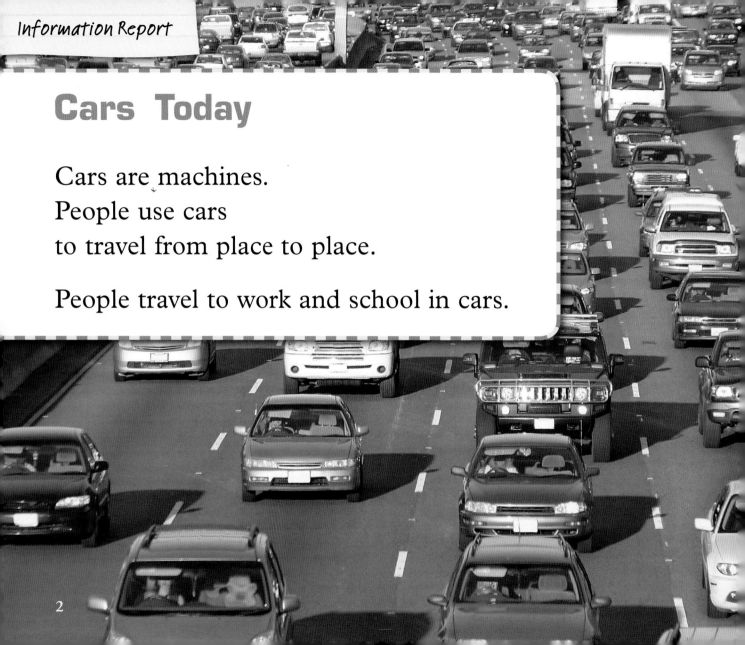

Cars Today

Cars are machines.
People use cars
to travel from place to place.

People travel to work and school in cars.

People travel to many other places in cars, too.

Some cars are big.
Big cars have big engines.
They carry lots of people and heavy loads.

Some cars are small.

Small cars have small engines.

They do not use as much petrol as big cars.

Today, cars are safer to drive
because they have better brakes and air bags.

Brakes help cars stop quickly.

Air bags help to keep people inside cars safe
in an accident.

brakes

air bags

Cars have seat belts.
The driver must wear a seat belt.
The passengers must wear seat belts, too.

Car seats help
to keep young children safe.

Sometimes, police check cars
to see if they are safe
to drive on the road.

POLICE

VEHICLE
SAFETY CHECKS

9

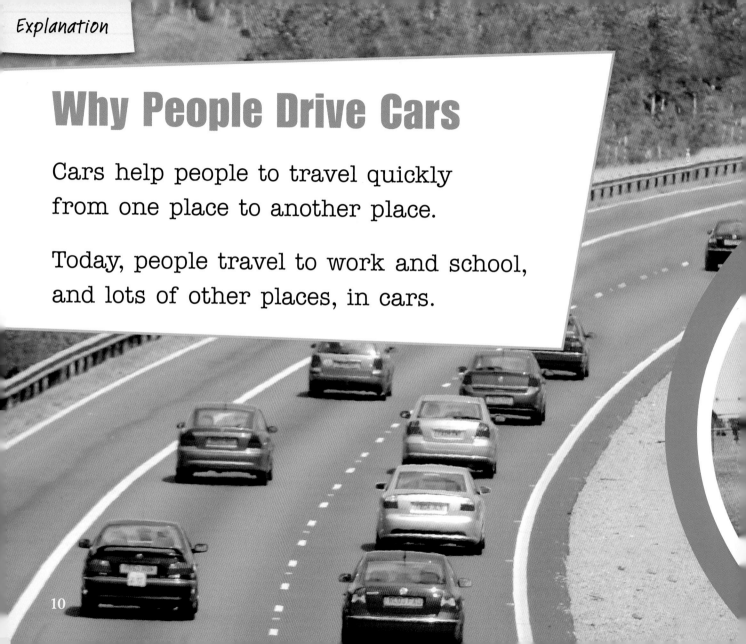

Why People Drive Cars

Cars help people to travel quickly from one place to another place.

Today, people travel to work and school, and lots of other places, in cars.

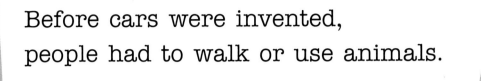

Before cars were invented,
people had to walk or use animals.

Some people drive big cars because they need to carry passengers or heavy loads.

Some people drive small cars
because they do not use much petrol.

13

Today, cars are much safer to drive.

Most cars have air bags and seat belts.
Air bags and seat belts
can stop people inside the car
from being hurt badly in an accident.

Cars help people to travel quickly and safely from one place to another.